The Sat Nav Guide to Your Soul

By Jeff Lloyd ©

A Manual to Help You Tune into Your Inner Guidance System

Foreword

It was in 2009 that the idea of this book first came to mind. For some years I had been channelling messages whilst meditating. I would sit quietly with a pen and paper and write down the thoughts that came into my head. I found out by meditation, that these words and their wisdom were channelled from a guide of mine called Aaron. I had quite a lot written down but didn't know how to put it together. Then one day, reading an advertisement in a local paper, I saw "Sat navs" for sale! That was it. In a flash I had the idea for the book, a guide book, just like a manual you would get with a new electrical device or phone. What if we all have an inherent, internal guidance system to help us on this mortal journey? A system that most of us don't know we have and don't know how to tune into to get the guidance we need? I jotted down a few outlines and ideas but then had to put it to one side because my life was changing fast and I was going through a huge transition. In retrospect, I could not have written it if the subsequent events and changes to my life had not taken place.

As you will discover it has been a long journey to get from the place I was in to writing these lines that are before you now!

From the first conception of the book I kept putting it to one side and leaving it. Then one evening in the summer of 2012, I went to Wigan Spiritualist church. I was new to the area and thought that at least I might meet like minded people there who believed that there is more to life than X Factor and soaps.

A lot of people go to these meetings, sometimes for months, hoping to get a message from a loved one they have lost. So I was surprised when a message came through for me via one of the mediums. The message was from my grandmother, Mary Ann who passed over when I was 10 years old.

For the sceptics amongst you, a good medium will give three to four pieces of information so that you can identify the spirit who is coming through to you. This he did, and then gave the main message my gran wanted to convey to me which was to finish the book I had started. Remember, no one knew me in the church as I was new to the area, never mind that I was trying to write a book.

I thought, Aaron is giving me these lovely messages from spirit and now he's had to send my poor old grandmother to come and give me a kick up the backside to get it finished. So I left with my tail between my legs and decided to knuckle down and to finally finish it off. Thanks Gran!

It is strange how, once you make a decision to do something, the universe moves quickly to get people and situations to pop into your life to help you get the job done. Since making that decision, I have met some lovely people, and made some good friends to whom I am forever grateful for helping me to finally get the book into print.

I am writing this in January 2013. 2012 has been and gone and yes, we are all still here which presumably means that all the people who made lots of money predicting the end of the world on the 21st of December 2012 will be looking in their diaries to see when the next disaster is going to strike us so that they can make even more cash based on people's fears.

Fear, that small, almost innocuous word that manifests itself constantly as it weaves its way in a variety of different forms through the media, press, and advertising. Even our friends, families and neighbours are quick to point to some negative, just in case we thought we were going to have a good day!

So this little hand book is your guide to break free of all that fear and negativity and to living a happy, prosperous and joyful life.......but you know that already don't you?

Also included in this book are the lyrics of two songs from the album "If Symptoms Persist," written by my son Denny Lloyd, which fit perfectly into the context of this manual. I have provided links to the songs if you wish to down load them which, of course, I recommend you do.

Thank you for reading these words although, of course, it was always meant to be. It has been a long and winding road for us to be together in this moment of time and space, in fact, it is an incredible feat of co creation between you and I and of course the universal consciousness. Any slight deviation and we would not be together now in this divine moment.

Our conscious thoughts create our lives and reality by ingraining into our subconscious minds our beliefs about who we perceive ourselves to be. The universal or super consciousness tunes into our subconscious minds and will do everything it can to create and make those beliefs, our reality.

Don't like your reality? Simple, change your thoughts!

In essence we are all one! Everyone we have met, every place we have been, everything which we have drawn into our lives, every word we have uttered or heard becomes part of the tapestry and colour of our life, either on a conscious or subconscious level and helps make us the wonderful beings that we all are!

Below are just a few of the souls that I have met and left during my journey and I give a special thanks to them all for making the tapestry of my life so magical and special!
Who would you put on your list?

In no special order:

My family, Mike and Mary, Steve Cambden, Paul and Philippa, Conrad, Sam, Carla, Jenny Parris, , Donald, John and Kate Hardman, Neil, Pat, Tony, Carol, Eddie and Liz Hardin, Nhojer, Jennifer Clayton, Sharon de Rose, Lyn and Nick Bunce, Eileen Long, Michelle, Helen, Miss Jones, Marie Webster, Julie Edwards, Anna and Gemma Taylor, Foggy, Linda Love, Dodgy Steve Sandi Teale, Maurice, Vanessa, Marilyn, Elaine, Jenny, Leanne, Mo and Katie Peter, George and Jean, Rachel, Natalie, Hope Solanus Mr Wilkes, Spid, Felicity, Shirley White, Big Jules, Steve Lewis, Lloyd.

Special thanks to; Julie English, for back cover photograph and support, Barbra Forber, "Barberra" Scott, Alice Bower and Jenny Parris (for her art work of the Om on the back cover, plus tea sympathy, soup and encouragement when it was needed most!) for helping me make this book part of my "reality" and of course not forgetting Aaron for "inspiration"

Dedicated to Ruby, Who is? And continues to be an inspiration to all our family!

The Meaning (Denny Lloyd)

Though the meaning is not clear, there's a reason why we're here
Though we don't always understand, well that's all part of the plan
To discover who we are, each of us has a unique part
Not knowing exactly where we start, or exactly where we'll go
Tell me which way I should go. Wonder where it is I'll go.

One day you may catch the eye of a stranger passing by
And your worlds they will collide who knows where you will arrive
Further down the path of time you never know what you might find
And though the road it twists and turns there's so much for you to learn
Tell me what am I to learn? Tell me lord when will I learn?
There's always a lesson to be learned I wonder if we'll ever learn?
Coz every body's on the run In fear of the things that have yet to come
But maybe we've only just begun and the light will shine on everyone
We've only just begun

God has left us on the ground for us to see what can be found
No matter which path we may choose there is nothing we can lose
Because what you choose to believe is just the perception of what you perceive
Just look at all we have achieved who ever thought we'd come this far?
Never dreamt we'd come this far how did we ever drift so far? There's no distance that's too far

Were so close but yet so far! Lord we're adrift so far! Lord we're adrift so far!
Lord we're adrift so far! So close yet so far!

Lyrics and music by Denny Lloyd © Available on iTunes visit www.dennylloyd.com
Visit denny lloyd on you tube

Beginning My Journey

When does the journey of the soul really begin? Is it at conception? When we are in the womb? When we are born? Or are we part of a divine omnipotent intelligence and consciousness and, subsequently, what we believe to be our soul has always existed and will always continue to exist as an infinite part in the mind of its creator? Do we choose our parents and the circumstances of our birth? Is it just by random chance? Or are we on some Karmic wheel, paying off our debts from other lives until the wheel no longer spins?

These are profound questions that theologians, seers and lay men have pondered over for Centuries and will probably do so for many more centuries to come. So being no expert and just a layman, I thought I would explain how I came to write this book and how I came to my own understanding of whom we are and where we are from. So it is best I start from where I know I began my journey in this life.

It was in the month of September 1952 that I was born and duly arrived in the city of Liverpool. I was a few weeks premature. Though why? I should be in such a rush to get here, I am not sure. Liverpool was still on its knees recovering from the Second World War, being the next most bombed English city after London.

Although we Liverpudlians are renowned for our sense of humour, I must give credit to the person who named the street that I was taken home to in the Edge Lane district of Liverpool. He must have had a great sense of irony. The street was called Pleasant View. The house was a two up two down Victorian slum terrace, which backed onto numerous other terraces, which were intersected by alleyways or "back entries" as we called them.

There was no inside toilet, no running hot water or central heating then, just one small coal fire in the main living room to heat the entire house. The main room had an ill fitting window and front door where, on a cold winters' day the winds' icy fingers would eagerly and easily dance their way between the gaps provided for them and chase their way straight through the house disappearing out of the ill fitting backdoor and windows, taking what little heat we had with it!

The street was surrounded by many similar terraces all purposely built for the incumbents to have just a short walking journey to the foreboding factories that employed them. The factories and the houses combined together to billow out their thick poisons and acrid smoke on its unsuspecting population creating the infamous yellow smog which would descend periodically to blanket out the sky and the entire city, taking what little air and daylight we had, causing many deaths due to illnesses such as asthma and bronchitis.

Liverpool, with its generations of immigrants from all over the world, was predominantly Catholic. We, on the other hand were Protestant which as far as I was concerned, was the much better deal. We only seemed to go to church on the religious festivals like Christmas, Easter and Harvest Festival, unlike my Catholic friends who seemed to have to go to mass at least once a day! If they missed a mass they would have to have a really good excuse to give to the priest when he visited their house on a Friday.

Friday was traditionally pay day for working families and the local Priest would duly appear for his bottle of Guinness and a donation to the church. Even then, at my tender years, I thought it odd that one of the richest organizations in the world could readily take money off people who had so little. It was with this oppressive religious back ground in which I lived my early childhood.
The image I had of God was the one that was generally bandied about in those years that of an elderly white man with a balding head and a flowing white beard. This God of love, peace and understanding it seemed had a bad temper and a big ego and was likely to send a bolt of lightning to incinerate you or turn you into a pillar of salt should you happen to upset him enough. So I guess it just might have been the fear factor that kept me in line and in awe of him and not the thought of receiving his unconditional love.

By the mid sixties the city was changing. The old slum terraces were being cleared and demolished and replaced with new housing and what were to become the monstrous high rise blocks of flats and maisonettes. Yes, it really was true. Where the might of the Nazi Luftwaffe failed to succeed in destroying Liverpool, the town planners and city council were finishing the job off for them.
It was not long before we were moved out of our slum terraces to one of the awful high rise blocks in the Lee Park district of the city. Of course it was not just the housing and restructuring of Liverpool that was happening. There were other stirrings in Liverpool during the early sixties.

Throughout my childhood music was an incredible influence and was always around me. Nobody had much money but everyone; it seemed, could either sing, had an instrument or could knock out a tune, whether it was on a guitar, piano, banjo, ukulele, accordion, washboard or even a set of spoons. Add this to the influence of music from the United States and the rest of the world, which was brought in from the seamen and seafarers who constantly came and went through the port. It was not surprising therefore; that there was a spontaneous eruption and the arrival of what became known as the Mersey Beat with its many bands, singers and comedians that came to the fore.

There was one band of course, that surpassed them all, The Beatles. So much has been written about them that I can only speak of the influence they had on me and how their music and influence shaped my thoughts about my life and spirituality during that time. I was just fifteen when in 1967, the so called summer of love and the Beatles psychedelic period came to the fore. I guess the two songs of theirs that really changed how I thought about life and started me searching for my own spirituality and questioning my own beliefs were, firstly, a song on the Sgt Pepper's Lonely Hearts Club Band Album called "Within you without you" by George Harrison. It was this Indian influenced song which most people probably skipped playing at the time and perhaps still do even now! It may have not been one of his most commercial songs but it was certainly one of his most profound. I would recommend anyone who has not really heard of it, or taken much notice of the lyrics, to go and have another listen to it.

The other song was Lennon McCartney's "All you Need is Love." The title of the song itself says all you need to know about spiritual truth. There is nothing else to add! After all, religions speak of God as love and love as being God! I believe it is man's interpretation on this statement that causes the confusion. We make everything to do with love conditional. "I'll only give you my love if you do this" or, "if you're a good boy or a good girl only then, will God love you!"

This period brought to the attention of the west, via the mass media, the eastern philosophy of meditation and re-incarnation. Life, it states, is just an illusion and the reality is that we are spiritual beings in a temporary vehicle called physical body which we use like a car to get ourselves around on the earth plane. Then when we have experienced what we came here for, it's off we go back to the spirit realms to consider the next vehicle and the next journey and circumstances that we would like to undertake!

This made far more sense to me than fearing that awful old man up in the sky with his long beard and big book of judgment and threats of locusts and lightning bolts. So I guess this was the first real turning point and change of direction on my own road of discovery or rediscovery. By changing my perspective, and the way I viewed my reality, I now believe I had left one possible road and journey, with its many possibilities, behind and created another with its own twists and turns and eventualities for myself.

My first odd or mystical experience (if that is the right term) of my adult life came when I was about 20 years old. I was lying in bed one night suffering from a really heavy cold and feeling rather sorry for myself. In between that moment of wakefulness and falling asleep I felt myself float out of my body and I could see myself lying on the bed. I felt so good and at peace being out that awful sick body. Then I suddenly got frightened and, as soon as I feared I might be dying or might not be able to get back, instantly I was back in my body.

Looking back I just wish I had known what I know now and realized that I was astral travelling or having an out of body experience (OBE) and then I would have been able to embrace the experience.

The second experience around about the same time happened when a few friends and I were walking through a local wood called The Nook in Gateacre. Although it had a reputation for being haunted I had been through it many times before without witnessing anything remotely spooky, but on this occasion we saw a white ghostly figure wandering through the wood. Being in a group gave us more bravado than we might otherwise have had if we had been on our own and we chased after it, but it moved too fast for us and disappeared off into the night. I often wonder what would have happened if it had stopped, turned around and chased us? What would we have done?

Of course, no one believed us about what we had experienced and that is always the problem with this sort of phenomenon. Unless you produce hard evidence no one ever takes you seriously and, if you do, it is usually dismissed as fake.

It was not long after that incident in the spring of 1974 that I decided to leave Liverpool. I was in my early twenties and became somewhat depressed and disillusioned having been working a "soul" destroying shift rotation system for over two years in Dunlops, a local tyre factory in Speke. Fearing this was my life for the next forty years or more I decided to leave and seek my fame and fortune in the south of England

After stopping off in many of the southern coastal towns I ended up in Southsea, a small seaside town just outside Portsmouth. It was there I met Lyn, my wife to be. We decided to move in together and shared a room in a large house but we quickly found we were not alone. We were also sharing the room with a ghost (whom we fondly called "Icky"). Although we never actually saw anything it would make its presence felt by sometimes turning on taps in the middle of the night. It also had a habit of opening drawers, the wardrobe and cupboard doors.

After a few months together Lyn and I decided to return to Liverpool (leaving "Icky" behind). However, we both struggled to find work. I did eventually manage to get a job with Liverpool parks and gardens, working at Bowring Park Golf Course. Lyn was from the south of England and continued to find it hard to settle and even harder to find work. So in the late seventies, as Liverpool's industrial base was virtually shutting down due to recession, we decided to head back down to the South of England and build a new life for ourselves there.

Our first job was a joint position. Lyn worked as a nanny and I worked as a gardener at a place called Denchworth Manor, set in the beautiful Oxford countryside near Wantage. The original part of the property is mentioned in the Doomsday Book which was compiled in 1086 AD. Although we were only there a relatively short time we still witnessed many strange happenings, the first of which began on our very first night!

As the previous Nanny and gardener were still occupying the apartment that went with the job for several more days we were hastily put in the newly converted barn, called the Wool Store, where monks had once stored their wool and which had been standing almost as long as the house. It was beautifully refurbished with touch tone lighting and modern designer furniture, with the bedroom situated on the newly constructed musicians' gallery which overlooked the whole of the inside of the barn.

It was a warm, still summer evening as I began to unpack the final few boxes and belongings from the car. Being city born and bred I was amazed how incredibly quiet and peaceful it was and how beautiful the stars looked, twinkling like diamonds and gems in the clear, cloudless night sky without the pollution or glare of street lighting to obstruct them. I removed the final box of possessions from the boot of the car and closed the heavy oak door of the barn behind me.

Tired and exhausted, Lyn and I were both looking forward to sleeping in our temporary but luxurious accommodation. As it turned out sleep would be the last thing that we would get that night. As soon as we got into bed and turned off the light, there was a loud knocking on the oak door. It startled us both and sounded really urgent. So I quickly put on some clothes and ran down the stairs. I unbolted the door and as soon as it began to open the knocking stopped. I pulled it wide open only to find nobody there! I looked outside but could see no one. It was strange as no one could have run away in the short time it took to open it!
Rather bemused I shut the door but no sooner had it closed than the knocking began again. I was about to re open it when Lyn shouted down to draw my attention to the huge, heavy Victorian mirror that hung on the far wall and was now swinging from side to side. I ran back up the stairs with the sound of heavy footsteps following not far behind me. By now the windows had also decided to join in the crescendo, somehow managing to rattle and shake even though there was no wind or breeze outside to disturb them.

As we sat on the edge of the bed, both of us shaking and wondering what to do, one of us remembered that we had bought The Radha Krishna Mantra Album off one of the many Hari Krishna people that frequented the high street in Oxford at that time. Thinking that this energy, or whatever it was that was causing the disturbance, just might not like the sound of mantras and having no better plan other than to run screaming into the night, we summed up all our combined courage and then I followed Lyn down stairs (ladies first of course!) past the persistent banging on the door, and the swinging mirror on the wall, and quickly found the record and started to play it at full volume. After several plays of the Hari Krishna Mantra and with us singing along as loud as possible for what seemed an age everything suddenly stopped! It had worked!

It was quite some time before we tentatively went back up the stairs to try to sleep. Although this was the most dramatic episode of our stay there were many other strange happenings of which there are too many to mention here. I can't say that we weren't relieved to leave there after only a few months. Looking back it was almost as though some force did not want a couple, who believed in light, universal love and meditation, cramping its style and did everything it could to make our stay as uncomfortable and as eventful as possible!
We then moved to Windsor and later to Sunningdale. Although Lyn and I never had much money we were blessed with lots of love for each other and in 1979 we were

joined by the arrival of our lovely son Denny. We had our own form of spirituality, being vegetarian, living our simple philosophy of meditation, love and pacifism and not adhering to any particular form of religion or worship.

In the early eighties we were doing our bit for the peace movement. Going to the American air base at Greenham Common to protest against cruise missiles, taking part in CND marches in London and anything else we could do to promote peace and love.

During this time we also enjoyed our great love of music, playing the local pubs and recording songs in a local studio owned by our now good friend John Hardman, whose young daughter Sarah (later to be known as Sarah Harding of Girls Aloud) would often play together with our son Denny. In fact many years later in the summer of 1999 Denny and I did a gig in Sunningdale at the Chequers Pub and were joined by John on guitar and the then 17 year old Sarah on vocals just before her rise to "stardom."

The one period of my life in which, I feel that I lost my spirituality and belief came during the mid eighties, which was when I was brought down to earth by a painful divorce. In the spring of 1983 Lyn and I had just started a combined job of Head Gardener/Housekeeper in Sunningdale when she suddenly announced that she had met someone else. I was devastated.

Later in this book I talk about "what is reality?" Anyone who has been through a major shock or trauma will know what I mean when I say that the whole experience seemed almost surreal, like a waking dream or nightmare, not being able to grasp or take in the events or what is happening to you. Perhaps it was because, like a lot of couples, on the surface you convince yourself that everything is fine and you ignore things that do not flow any more, or that are not quite right. Instead of talking and facing up to them, you allow things to drift on until it becomes too late.

Maybe it was also because we married when we were very young and began to drift apart and to pull in different directions instead of growing together. We spent the next year trying to stay together but this only made us both even more unhappy. Lyn became pregnant and three months into the pregnancy had a life threatening miscarriage. The strain on both us, as well as on Denny, was too much and we decided the best thing to do was to separate.

I became completely disillusioned with life. I went from what was once a happy marriage to becoming a divorcee and reluctantly having to become a weekend only father to my son Denny. Subsequently I lost my highly paid job as Head Gardener and the luxury apartment on an estate owned by a wealthy Arab family in Sunningdale that went with it.

This left me full of anger and resentment and I lost my way spiritually for at least the next ten years. After all I thought, "What had I done to deserve all this crap?" Maybe there was, after all, that old bald bloke with the white beard up there in the sky now taking out his revenge for me not believing in him. Although there have never been any great flashes of lightning or visions or a "road to Damascus moment" (and I was always a bit envious of those people who claimed to have had them) I must admit that I have always felt I was never alone.

No matter how hard I pushed my old beliefs away I always felt there was something more. Even in my "Dark Night of the Soul Moments" of which there have been several in fact, I found that when I came through those times I always felt I was renewed with a greater inner strength and realization and vision. I always felt as if there was some divine or supreme entity not outside of me but within, guiding and enlightening me, although it was a long time before I felt at one with it.

I have spent most of my working life (about 30 years) close to nature working as a gardener. So please don't talk to me about carbon foot prints. The amount of trees and shrubs I have planted over the years I could probably go around the solar system twice before I use up all my fuel credits. Working as a gardener it has always amazed me how nature has its own intelligence. The plants, birds and animals know instinctively how to behave, what to do and when to do it. The Earth herself has her own intelligence and knows its relationship with the animals and plants in its care. I believe the Earth herself is a living breathing entity.

Our ancestors knew this, as did the great tribes of the Americas, Africa and Australia which is why they revered the seasons and what the land yielded for them, unlike most of us now who are completely detached, and the multinational companies of today that extract her minerals and, in return, pollute her for profit and, of course, not forgetting the "mad axe men" in the South American rain forests who are cutting down her lungs which enable us all to breathe as quickly as they can. We humans are only just waking up to the fact that we cannot continually just keep taking from the land and systematically pollute the environment and the Earth without storing up many problems for ourselves in the future. As for nuclear power, how insane is it to use a fuel that cannot be contained when something goes wrong, as is happening now in Fukushima Japan?

We have to have a symbiotic existence with the Earth. I believe that whatever we take out we should also give back in return. This is known in eastern philosophy as the universal spiritual law of Karma. This is law of action and reaction. It works not unlike Isaac Newton's law of motion, which is that for every action there is an equal and opposite reaction. So whatever action you take now it will ultimately come back and reflect or react upon you.

During the late 1980's and 1990's I became self employed and worked the gardens for an array of many different people, from old age pensioners who would be desperately upset if they were not in to pay you the small amount they owed, to the rich, and sometimes famous, who, it would appear, would do anything they could not to part with their money and pay you, or at least not on time! Sunningdale, Ascot and Wentworth are some of the most expensive and exclusive areas of England and the late eighties saw the rise of the so called yuppies, people who earned money hard and fast then spent it just as quickly.

I look back at that period with mixed emotions. It was the worst time of my life, on one hand, as I was going through a divorce, but on the other hand, it was also the best. Playing in a local band I met lots of famous people as many of them frequented a local pub called the Red Lion. It wasn't unusual to see Diana Dors, Ringo Starr, Barbra Bach, Rod Stewart, Rick Wakeman, Denny Laine and Sam Fox from the music world and comedians such as Jim Davidson and Russ Abbott. Zak Starkey would occasionally drum for us as he didn't have a band. It seems funny now, as he went on to play for The Who and Oasis.

Zak invited me to his 21st birthday party at John Lennon's former home, Tittenhurst Park, which Lennon had given to Zak's dad, Ringo Starr, when Lennon and Yoko went to live in New York! It was at that party that I met amongst other famous people, Paul McCartney. Paul, on hearing my accent came over and started chatting to me. After asking me what I did for a living, I cheekily asked what he did, to which he laughingly replied "I'm a musician". I looked to his wife Linda, smiled and said, much to her amusement, "He'll never make a living out of it. He should get a proper job." When Ringo Starr eventually sold Tittenhurst Park my friend and I got the contract to maintain the garden of his new property on Chobham Common, Surrey, until he eventually sold it and moved to Monaco.

It was during these heady times of meeting the rich and famous that I got working in a small property in Sunningdale. It was owned by an Austrian woman called Helen who was a medium and who also read Tarot cards. I would sometimes barter my gardening skills in exchange for a reading from her. I remember she gave me a reading not long after my father died and she told me things about him and our relationship no one else outside of the family would have known. She also told me he kept repeating "They have got my money." This mystery was solved a few weeks later when his old company admitted they had short changed his pension and reimbursed the money which my mother was only too glad to receive. I think this was when I first started to believe again that perhaps there was something beyond us and this mortal coil and started to look outwardly to fill the emptiness or void that I had felt for so long.

Due to the economic crash or "Black Monday" as it was called in 1987 my work plummeted and my mortgage doubled almost overnight. This was the end of the easy, fast money of the eighties in the South of England. The Porsches, which were once the favoured status symbol of the so called "yuppies", were now two a penny to buy and the credit cards which helped to wine, dine and fuel many a festive occasion and bloated lunches were now cut in half!

I was getting deeper and deeper into debt as house prices crashed and buyers were few and far between. I struggled on for the next three years trying to sell my house and getting deeper into debt. Finally, in 1991, I got a buyer and after paying off the money I owed to the bank I came away with the princely sum of £400 but at least the mind numbing pressure of being over £40,000 in debt was lifted.

It was then I made the next big move of my life. Unable to afford to rent anywhere in the Sunningdale, Ascot area, I rented a friend's flat about 10 miles away in Knaphill, Woking. This was another low point of my life. Denny, who was now about 12 years old, was living in Thame, Oxfordshire. If the three hour round trip to pick him up wasn't bad enough driving in my old, battered, barely legal Ford Cortina Estate made it even more precarious. Still, we managed to spend one weekend a month together and had more time in the school holidays. The periods in-between were very lonely and I felt really isolated, especially as I had stopped playing in the band and didn't know anyone at all in Woking

It was around the mid-nineteen nineties that the next major shift on my journey happened! Having had this feeling of emptiness and that something was missing in my life for so long now I started to ask the great and wonderful creator, universe or whatever it liked to call itself if it really did exist to show me a way, give me a sign and show me a way forward. Sure enough, when scouring the local Guildford college prospectus one of the courses caught my eye and jumped out of the page at me. Although I cannot remember the exact wording it spoke about healing and self healing and finding that inner self and light that I felt I had extinguished all those years ago!

It was a course on Colour Healing and psychology run by a lovely lady and now good friend, Eileen Long. It not only opened up to me a whole new world of Colour Therapy, Auras, and Chakras but also one of spirituality, hands on healing and distant healing. It was here on this course that I met my partner to be, Jenny, who for the next ten years would also be my best friend and confidante. Jenny helped and encouraged me to train in Hypnosis, Past Life Regression, Spirit Release and EFT (Emotional Freedom Technique.)

Taking the Colour Healing course changed my view and perspective on life completely. It encouraged me to think "outside the box," and not to believe all the currently held and accepted beliefs and conventions of the establishment. After all, the world isn't flat, as the early sea pioneers such as Columbus proved. So, too, Galileo was right, although pilloried at the time for claiming that the Earth does orbit the Sun and not the other way round as the church in that time would have everybody believe.

During the Christmas period of 1999, whilst living alone, I caught influenza. No not the man flu but the real deal. I was unable to get out of bed, having a high fever and aching joints. Having asthma too only made it worse, making it really difficult to breathe. I was laid up for over a week. Whilst lying in my bed and feeling so ill, thinking that perhaps dying might be a really good option, I started to hear voices in my head. The voices came through slowly at first. They spoke with an old English accent, sort of Shakespearian. I jotted down a lot of what they were saying. Some of the words and statements were quite deep and profound. After a few days they were getting overwhelming and annoying so I asked them in no uncertain terms to leave and, whoever they were, they certainly got the message as they went away and to date, have never come back.

I subsequently used some of the words and ideas they gave me in my first little book of thoughts; "Beyond the rainbow" which I published in 2002.It was at this time that I read, Conversations with God by Neil Donald Walsch, which profoundly changed my way of thinking about reality. The God in his book asks us to consider, what if it wasn't all by chance? What if we really do create our own reality by what we think, speak and do?

From 2001 to 2009 I was living in East Horsley with my partner Jenny. It is a small but very affluent village just outside Guildford, Surrey. Although I was still gardening, after 30 years it was beginning to take its toll on my body. I developed arthritis in my hip which gave me continual pain, had a slipped disc in my back and had "tennis elbow" in each of my arms. It was during these years that I realized I needed to get out of horticulture before my body wore out completely.

So, with the encouragement and great support of Jenny, I studied hard. Firstly, I took a hypnosis course on how to take people into Past Life Regression and release spiritual attachments. I followed this up with Hypnosis and then EFT. Together we also ran workshops and developed a small meditation group which we held at our home once a week.

During some sessions of past life regression done under hypnosis, I have come across spirits that have attached themselves to an individual. This can occur for many reasons. Usually the person has suffered from depression, been in hospital (always a good place to find a displaced spirit) or even attached themselves from another life time. They can be removed quite easily. Far from the nightmare scenario a priest might put you through, casting out demons with their book and the bells approach, the spirits quite often don't know that they have passed over and are only too keen to be helped toward the light. It's quite funny, too, sometimes hearing people talk in a totally different dialect, as the spirit has to speak through someone else's vocal chords.

Typically, the only time I got really worried was probably the time I came across an attachment with one of my first clients. He was quite a tall man with a big physique. He sat down and as I put him under hypnosis, he gave off all the classic signs of having an attachment. I informed the spirit that I knew of its presence, so it might as well speak to me and I would send it on its way. If they own up too easily you can be sure these are lesser spirits who go to the light meekly and easily. If this happens there is usually another entity behind them with a much bigger ego. Sure enough several came out and identified themselves quite quickly and I duly sent them on their way. I then set about tackling the much bigger entity hiding behind them as they always send the menials out first hoping they will not be found. So I said "OK, that's got rid of those poor souls, so you can now come to the fore and speak with me. It's no good hiding, I know you're there!" The client who was still sitting in the chair under hypnosis, almost a passive observer as to what was going on suddenly turned his head towards me and said with a deep, gruff, rasping voice a Boris Karloff monster would be happy to make and said "And just what has it got to do with you? Who do you think you are? To tell me what I should do" The fact that this was one of my first clients and I was inexperienced and he was such a big man with a heavily built frame only gave the voice more gravitas. The hairs stood up on the back of my neck and every other place I had them! My immediate thought was to ask myself if we had a bible in the house. The second was to just run out the door and leave him and the client to it? Luckily my training kicked in and I confronted him. Funny, as I now realize from experience, once you face up to them, they quickly drop the aggressive tone and usually tell you what an awful life they have had and are so happy to go on to the light with their loved ones and leave the Earth plane behind. The client, who had only come to see me because he wanted to stop smoking, came out of hypnosis completely bemused and, happily for him, a non smoker.

I have also experienced many amazing healings, way beyond the realm of understanding of conventional medicine. I have seen and witnessed people recover totally after being given "hands on healing" for an illness for which their own doctor had indicated that the best course of action was to go home and await their fate! When confronted with these types of healings the medical profession calls it "Spontaneous remission" as they have no way of accepting anything outside of their paradigm. This is because they only deal with two states of the human condition, the physical and the mental. They see the body in the Newtonian way as a two dimensional mechanical machine that sometimes breaks down and needs repairing by drugs or surgery rather than looking at it as a multi-dimensional system having physical, mental, emotional and spiritual levels, all of which need to be addressed in order to encourage the body to use all of its resources to repair itself. I am convinced that when we go through an emotional trauma it will appear in the physical body at a later date and vice versa, when we have physical trauma it will eventually manifest in the emotional body.

I also tried my hand at automatic writing. This is a method to make contact with any spiritual guides that may want to connect with you. My own particular way of doing it was to empty my mind and let it go blank (family and friends will tell you I have a natural ability for this) then hold a pen over a piece of paper and write down whatever comes into my mind. By doing this I had a guide come through called Aaron. It is his words that you see in this book which are written in italics. It was also these words that gave me the inspiration for this book. Aaron, it turns out, lived with me in Egypt over 2000 years ago and has chosen to help guide me in this life. I was lucky enough to visit Egypt with a group of like minded friends. I must admit it really did feel like I had been there before; it all seemed very familiar and the ancient sites have an incredible energy about them.

In April 2008 I had booked a table in East Horsley Village Hall which was hosting a Mind Body Spirit fayre. These fayres are held so that holistic practitioners and others who do a variety of disciplines, or sell crystals, or give tarot or psychic readings can demonstrate their wares and attract new clients. The weather was atrocious and I doubt if more than three people turned up all day. Standing at the table next to me was an old friend and medium, Shirley White, who was a psychic and a member of the Woking Spiritual Church. As we were both completely bored and I had nearly emptied the tea urn, I turned to Shirley and asked her if she would mind giving me a tarot card reading, which she duly did. Now although I have seen and witnessed many a strange occurrence over the years and am completely open to all sorts of possibilities, I was so shocked by what she told me that the cynical part of me thought, "Mmm, I think you're making this all up as you go along." This was because she said I would be moving home, uprooting, starting all over again, living alone and would be really successful when I was living and working with people from my own background. I totally dismissed this as I felt really happy with where I was and my situation. I thanked her and I folded up the paper I had written the reading down on, put it in my pocket and placed it at the back of the chest of drawers in my bedroom and forgot all about it.

It was about a year later when the predictions from the reading started to unfold. My relationship with Jenny stated to change and although I felt we had always been close, after the turn of the year 2009 we started to become distant. Her trip to India only seemed to exasperate the situation. After staying in an Ashram for several weeks she returned with a new philosophy and meditation practices and our strained relationship changed totally and eventually it started to fall apart.

As our relationship deteriorated I remembered the tarot reading and could not believe that almost everything that was written down on that piece of paper at the back of the drawer was beginning to unfold. We finally separated in the November of 2009 and having little or no financial resources to enable me to stay in the Guildford area, and with my body creaking and aching like an old rusty gate, I decided to give up gardening completely and head back up to the north of England where the rest of my family lives. I was fortunate enough to have the love and support of all of my family and was able to stay with my sister Jean and her husband Barry for several months. I will always be indebted to them for it gave me the chance to rest, recoup and regroup my thoughts and feelings, before throwing myself fully into my healing work which, as predicted by Shirley, is proving to be very successful.

I am now in the north of England working with people from a similar background to myself. Since giving up gardening completely my health has improved considerably. No longer do I get any pain from my hip, arms or back. I put this down to rest, self healing and healing I have been given by the new friends I have made. Also, when you're in a job or situation that no longer serves you and you are not facing up to the fact that you need to change, the subconscious mind creates circumstances that leave you with no other choice than to make the necessary changes no matter how difficult they are at the time.

Although I believe that we are always where we have chosen to be on our journey, when looking back at that period in my life it may seem that perhaps some of those events were predestined. My own view is that every possibility is happening NOW! It was just that the tarot reader was picking up the echoes of one of many possible futures available to me. When viewing the journey I have made in my own life it is obvious that if I had made alternative choices or taken a different turning or decision then the road I would be on now would be entirely different. The irony of this, of course, is that with hindsight perhaps I would have made decisions to make my journey a lot easier. But then I might not be sitting where I am now, writing the pages of this book or doing the work I am doing - helping people to move forward with their lives!

So this is has been my journey so far and is how I came to write the following pages. Whether you agree or disagree with my views is fine by me, we all have a right to be and have our own opinions. It is of no importance. We all feel we are a long way from home, yet we are ever just a breath away. What really matters is to always remember that you are a part of the vast and wonderful "multi-verse" and that you being very small in comparison does not diminish your role, your significance or your greatness within it.

And who knows? Without you being part of it, it just might not exist at all!

"There is no beginning, as there is no end

No up, down, left or right or tricky bend

No place to get to, no place to leave

No time to kill or pattern to weave

It's all just illusion a trick of the mind

Only in stillness and silence will the answers you find"

Preparation for the journey

The soul was contemplating what it would be like to journey from its current state of being and knowing. Surrounded by love and enlightenment to the lower reaches and vibrations of the life it was about to undertake upon the earth. Asking its guide what path it should take, the guide answered; "Although many facets of your journey you have already decided, you'll find you tread the path that gives you the most wisdom" was the reply.

"How will I choose such a path?" it questioned.

"All paths lead to the same door. There is no right or wrong way to take. The only way is the right one for you at any given moment. You can create and co-create all your experiences with those with whom you choose to bring onto your journey.

Some you will have journeyed with before in other lives. Each thought, every action you take will weave the tapestry of your life. The challenges you face will be the ones you bring upon yourself.

Will they be difficult, hard, easy or sublime? It is entirely up to you how you choose to perceive them."

Your journey

So begins your journey on earth. You see many roads, twists and turns. Yet you find there are so few signs to guide you and the ones that you do see only seem to confuse you even more. You see many other travellers. Some are heading in your direction and others choosing a different route. Some just run around like headless chickens not knowing where they are going and without any sense of direction. Some act startled, like rabbits caught in the glare of the headlights of an oncoming car or like sheep (sheeple) they blindly follow the direction they are pointed in by others.

Confused, you can either keep to the course you are on, pull over and try to get directions or just keep on going and hope that eventually you will find a sign that will point you in the right direction.

In many ways it doesn't really matter which route you take as all roads will take you to your final destination.

There are many alternative roads that are open to you that you can take to make the journey you travel so much more agreeable and easy to travel. So there is no need to worry because I will explain how to use your inner guidance and how to connect you with The Sat Nav Guide to your Soul that will help guide and direct you.

After all, none of this is new. Ever since the dawn of his existence mankind has looked up to the stars, questioned and wondered where? Why? And when did he come into being! And what his role in the whole equation of existence is.

The problem has always been that the answer to these profound questions it would seem was always in the domain of a few highly select individuals who by birth, privilege or status would guide the ill informed masses to purgatory, their salvation or their damnation.

It was suggested by these few privileged people that only by denial of the flesh, the things you really like and enjoy; being humble; servitude or obedience, could you save your mortal soul. Whilst they, of course, indulged and gorged themselves in whatever they wanted to or fancied without any impunity from a higher deity.

In more recent times, especially in the West, it became popular to go to India and find yourself an Ashram and a guru who claimed to be the true master of enlightenment. You would either then give yourself, your body or your money (or preferably all three) over to him before he would take you up a mountain, sit you in painful positions and teach you some sacred yogic moves and mantras before giving you the secret wisdom of the ages.

Unfortunately too often people, like moths that are drawn to the light, are also drawn to the glow that appears to shine from others. This is because of their fear that they are inferior and become convinced that someone else is far wiser than they are and has all the answers to the questions they seek.

Thankfully none of this is true. You are the master and creator of your own journey. Everything you require for your journey here on Earth is within your reach. It requires no unpleasant bending, no spiritual master or doctrine or self denial. In fact the ways of the masters, such as Christ, Buddha, Allah and Krishna are usually misrepresented.
Power lies within us all. Why indeed go through the "middleman" when you can go straight to the top yourself? So do not doubt yourself or your neighbour, brother or sister. For that which is all embracing and encompassing is within reach of everyone. Behold love, it is such a small word for something that is so vast but what lies within it is infinite.

Love has the power to change all around it while it remains constant.
Love is the ultimate conqueror of all things, the spark in every flame.
All that is required of you is to do nothing at all but to be still, listen and make the greatest journey of all - the inner journey!

Our outer reality conforms to our beliefs and expectations. All knowledge and what we experience is a construct of our own thought and imagination. Our thoughts create our outer experience. Everyone experiences their reality differently.

Our consciousness is not out there or inside our minds but is everywhere and at one with the universal consciousness.
When we meet other people we interact with them on a conscious and sub-conscious level to conform to the other person's view of reality. This is how and why we attract other people into our lives to reinforce theirs and our reality.

We have no lessons or knowledge to learn for we are knowledge itself!
We do not have to learn how to love, for we are love itself! The Sat Nav Guide to your Soul will explain why you embarked on this great adventure and to help answer many of the questions you may have about your trip.
So sit back, relax and let your journey unfold!

Present Position

You are currently situated somewhere on a tiny planet known as Earth which is over ninety three million miles away from the nearest star known as the sun. The Earth is the third planet from the sun. Though you may feel you are standing still the Earth is actually rotating at an approximate equatorial speed of one thousand and forty miles per hour. On top of this the Earth is orbiting the sun at sixty seven miles per hour. At this speed it then takes the Earth over three hundred and sixty five days to complete its orbit.

The sun is part of a minor galaxy known as the Milky Way which consists of over a hundred billion stars and is a hundred thousand light years from side to side. It takes about two hundred million years for the Earth to orbit the centre of the galaxy.

The universe itself is expanding at over twelve million miles a minute.

"The vastness and beauty of the universe is small when Compared to the vastness and beauty within you all "

Welcome

You are a soul creating a human experience. What is a soul? It is an awareness of all objects and constructs. While all objects and constructs come and go the soul has always been and will continue to exist and observe. To put it another way, the soul is a small part of a universal consciousness that is having an experience or existence being human and to be human is to experience - happiness, pleasure, joy, sadness and suffering.

This universal consciousness can be likened almost to the internet. It is the source of all knowledge and everything that exists. It is always turned on and available to provide you with, and to down load to you, whatever information you wish to tune into it for. You are in possession of the most advanced unique guidance system available and it is ready to use at all times. Your Satellite Navigation, or Global Positioning System to the Soul, has been designed to tap into this great resource and make the journey in your vehicle (body) as easy to understand and enjoyable as possible. It is always present to guide and help you to where you want to be or go on your journey. Once you have been travelling and using it for a little while you'll probably have a good idea of what you can do, where you can go and what you can experience and how to perceive those experiences.

Support

Should you have any difficulties or need to know how to adjust, retune or get the best possible results out of your system, you'll find more details outlining its capabilities explained here.

Also, your guides are always on hand day and night twenty four seven to help point and assist you in the best direction that's right for you. All you have to do is ask! Even if you feel you can't always get through or it seems the lines are blocked, they are always there, guiding, sending messages, signals and signs to help you on your journey. The more you refine your system and the more you tune in the easier it is for you to receive their guidance.

"Hear not the words that are spoken but trust their meaning
See not what is in front of you but what lies within you

Speak not of the mind but from the heart
Listen only to those who gain nothing when speaking their truth"

Why do I need to make the Journey?

There is a consciousness or intelligence which is the driving force behind everything that is within and throughout the universe. This "ONE" consciousness or force also known collectively as God, Allah, Jehovah, our Lord, Krishna, the universe, plus a multitude of other names, created the journey so it could experience it's self subjectively! After all if there was only the "ONE" in existence how could it experience anything? Unless it divided itself into many different parts and forms.

It is this consciousness that is within every molecule, every atom, and every cell. It is the essence of all things. You are part of this essence, this life force and are part of the many facets of the "ONE". You are on the "ONE" journey! This is so that it might experience, by creating many aspects of itself. It is the breath of all life. Everything is created with intent. Be it from the seed to the flower, the acorn to the oak or the sperm to the egg. You are a vibration of this universal intelligence, part of that higher mind living on a lower vibration level of existence.
You are its thoughts and creation. So too, as you think, you also create the life you lead and the experiences you have. You are living in a narrow band of time and space reality, expressing and expanding your consciousness.

You experience duality - up/down, happy/sad, light/dark, birth/death, male /female, good /evil. You are a small but integral part of this mind matrix or living universal consciousness. It is forever changing and creating.
Every thought and action you have in turn affects everything and everyone, for all things are connected and interconnected by a field commonly known as the matrix. This is an invisible resonance or membrane that surrounds everything and through which passes all thought, knowledge and consciousness. The matrix holds together all matter and what you think and believe to be true.

You perceive what you create and weave the tapestry of your reality by your thoughts and the strength of emotion you place behind those thoughts.
The matrix or field of energy you are in is like a three dimensional hologram and like all holograms however much you divide or split it up, it always remains part of the whole and contains the "ONE" picture That is why whatever you do to another person you ultimately do to yourself and whatever you do unto yourself affects everything and everyone else.

As you make your journey you tend to identify yourself with your body and mind. Yet in truth they are not really you. The mind is only a receptor to the knowledge that is all around you .In fact you occupy many different bodies in one life time. Once you were the babe in arms, the toddler, the teenager, the adult and eventually the aged. They are just the vehicle and the method that you use to get you from A to B. Behind the "wheel" of this vehicle sits the driver or consciousness of the ONE!- forever guiding and nurturing you.

You, as part of these divine processes are on your way to find the way back home to become whole and integrated once again with this divine universal mind. What matters is not which road you take or how you find your way back home but the journey and experiences you undertake to get there!

Getting Started

It may surprise you to know this won't be the first time you have journeyed here. In fact you have lived and made this journey many times before, or to be completely accurate, you are living many lives in this one moment. For there is only ever one moment, now!

Time is not linear and does not exist as you perceive it. Imagine your lives to be like many different feature films in which you appear. Now imagine that all of these films are being shown and broadcast at the same time on countless channels and frequencies. Although you are not aware of the other films they are still there, still being broadcast and the lives being played out. You are not aware of them because you are only tuned in to this one at this moment.

This is how you evolve just like actors in a play, playing out your different roles. You use your body like a vehicle which seems to take us here and there, but what appears on the outside is really a reflection of what's happening on the inside. There is no left or right, up or down, right or wrong way to go. No past or future, only your consciousness which is creating that which is in front of you right now.

Sometimes you can get caught up in living your past thoughts wishing you had made different choices or decisions. This only brings sadness and guilt. You are not in that place any more. The actions you decided upon then were made by a different person with a different set of tools, values and life skills.

The past has gone and it only exists as a thought in your head and your perception of it. Once you change your perception of an event it can no longer influence you now or in the future as it did before.

Alternatively, you may constantly worry yourself thinking about how the future may unfold, which only leaves you in a state of fear! Both these states keep you in a lower vibration of thought and, as you will learn later, what you think you create!

Wherever you are, you are always here! You can only ever be here, now, in this moment! Remember if you went over there and you were asked where are you? The reply would be HERE! And the time would be NOW! So therefore it is always up to you how you view this moment and whether the situation is good, bad, indifferent or INSPIRING!

You are only ever aware of just a small expression of the vastness of who you really are. Within you are the resources of the universe! Each lifetime you have experienced is influencing who you are now and what you are going to create in the future! You are the driver, the navigator and the observer of the road you are on.

You have guides and helpers. These are beings of a higher vibration that also may have had many life times on the earth and have now chosen to remain free of the earth plane to guide others.

Before you set off you will have decided, with the help of your guides, the right vehicle (body) that suits you best, such as male or female. Which colour, special features, talents and other attributes? Then the location and circumstances which you feel will align you to your journey, plus the people (parents) who will best prepare you for what lies ahead. All this will have been meticulously planned before you set off.

SETTING OFF

Once you set off and enter this world on your journey of having a human experience the soul may become lonely or afraid. This is only because at birth we pass into the lower, denser vibrations of the earth plane. So it will forget that it is part of the "One" that creates all things. This is so it can experience life anew without any ties or attachments to previous existences.

Occasionally some souls can remember their past experiences and will often talk of different lives and places and countries they have lived.

There are many well documented cases where children experience this. They may even speak fluently in languages they are unfamiliar with but these memories usually fade by the seventh year of their journey (life). This is because by then they are so distant from the highest vibration they left at birth and the inevitable conditioning by their current circumstances and people around them.

Each soul chooses before birth the road which will give it the greatest experience. This is not necessarily the easiest one. We always have free will to change our route or direction at any given moment. It also co-creates all its experiences with other souls it chooses to meet on its path. So be bold, be strong, indeed why choose to be any different? For fear is always outside of you. Only love is within you. Each one has access to the power, creation and the wisdom of the ages, which is ingrained in every strand of our DNA and being, to make the choices that are right for us and our journey.

STREET GUIDANCE

This is the system you learn on the journey.
It relates to your experiences and how you interpret them. The three most important questions you can ever ask yourself are, "Who am I? Where am I? Where am I going?"
Sadly most people never ask these questions. Instead they choose lives of mediocrity. Their only escape is to live their own lives through the lives of other people or their so called hero without realising they can be the genius, the hero and inspiration in their own life.

Unfortunately, most people's view and perspective on life comes from the constant bombardment of the senses by the media, press, television, politicians, religion and the greedy leaders who impose their reality upon them.
They have no wish to convey the truth or keep you informed. It is more to do with keeping you in fear, control and guilt, which are dense, lower vibrations thus keeping you and everyone else in their control and their way of thinking!
The street guidance is also easily influenced when you are in a hypnotic like state watching TV or any other forms of the fear based media. It gets you to make decisions that are not necessarily leading you to take the easiest route.
When watching powerful emotional images, say of a disaster or terror attack, you are at your most vulnerable to be influenced because when staring at a TV screen you are in a trance like state. You become mesmerised by what you are seeing. In this state you are more likely to believe what you are being told or what is being portrayed to you.

The media leads by your fears and emotions and desires which can never be fulfilled. This is because once you have attained what you desire you find that it does not fulfil you.
The street guidance will then set new co-ordinates and drive you on to the next desire, then another.

It is only when you realise that it is this desire and attachment to the things that are outside of you that causes the most pain, can you let go and focus on the truth that lies within you.

There are two parts to the brain, the left hemisphere and the right hemisphere.
You are taught from an early age to think mainly from your practical left "male" brain, which deals with logic, facts, language, reasoning, detail and science and discouraged not to pay too much attention to your right "female" brain which deals with feelings, expression, reading, emotions, intuition, symbols, creativity, music, images and philosophy. It is the left side that dominates most of your life and the way you behave.
It is by listening more to the right female brain that you can allow yourself to become more balanced and compassionate towards others.

The street guidance also refers to the conscious and subconscious minds. The conscious mind is your creative mind and your personality which gives you your own individuality.
The subconscious is the link between the universal mind and the conscious mind. It also acts like a hard drive on a computer or like a recording device which uploads all your experiences. The basic programme for this life is uploaded from when you are in the womb and up until you are about seven years old.
Up until that age you are in a theta delta or trance like state so you accept the world as it is represented to you without rational conscious judgement. What is implanted then helps to construct your beliefs, your values, your fears and your view of the world around you.

So what is pre programmed in your early years of setting out - by parents, peers, siblings, teachers and friends - remains with you. About ninety six percent of all your responses and actions throughout your life are based on this pre programming within the subconscious.

"To master the gentle art of love
One must give without reward"

ACTIVE ROUTE GUIDANCE

Our real wisdom is quite often lost in this illusion we call reality. What is reality? It is the perception of what is happening outside of us. It really is what we make it. No person experiences reality, or creates reality, in the same way. Ask any two people or family members to remember an event in the past and you'll find they have a different memory or account of what happened. Some believe only what they see and hear, feel, touch and taste! Others what they are told to believe and others only what they are told to experience!

After all, people have been laying down their lives for centuries for what they believed to be a true and just cause only for history to give a totally different aspect or view on it. Don't forget history is written by the victors, not the losers, and therefore it is always has a biased account of events.

Our hearts beat out to the rhythm that all souls recognise - love - which is the purest vibration and most melodic of all melodies. Those who hear and feel this vibration are in harmony with all things. Unfortunately because of the pressure and stress of modern day life most have lost touch with this vibration. We put ourselves under so much pressure that we don't always listen to it or experience it. When we feel we are not going in the right direction we lose our rhythm and our way.

We all have the duality of the two voices within us. The brain contains our duality consciousness, of the left and right hemispheres, and gives us the voices which can give us a hard time and beat us up as often as we let it. This voice reinforces our limiting thoughts and beliefs and perception as to how we can, or should, create our lives.

Then there is the "other voice", the one we know comes from the heart. The one that gives us loving and compassionate thoughts, the one that gives us a "knowing" without having to weigh things up. The one we call our "gut feelings" or our intuition. The one we have been trained not to listen to and not to take notice of. This is our inner guidance. This is the one which connects us to our sat nav guidance. It is the voice of our hearts, our higher mind or higher self. When listening to the higher self it connects with the soul and as every soul knows its journey, its purpose and life path, it can then give you directions and the guidance you require. It is when we are going through stress or emotional issues that we misjudge these signals and we can seem to act irrationally or on impulse.

The heart is the beacon that ultimately connects us with the divine consciousness, so listen to it carefully.

"Only when you see another's fears will you feel their pain
Only when you feel their pain will you know thy heart!
Only when you know thy heart will you touch their soul!"

MAKING CHANGES

It is the structures that you build into your life that will ultimately define you. Yet everything you tell other people that you are and everything that you think you believe yourself to be is, in fact, an illusion.
For something to be real it has to have substance and as the mind has no substance the mind itself cannot be real.
Quantum physic states that the life you perceive with your five senses is not reality, only your perception of it. Your belief system determines what you see or believe to be true.
The world outside of you only mirrors what is happening to you on the inside.
Only when focusing your consciousness on something and giving it your intent does it enter your reality?

Beliefs can be changed in an instant and you can make changes to your journey at any time. By changing your thoughts and intent you also change your energy and vibration.
You are energy, existing in a world of vibration.
At the time of the big-bang, all energy and forces were unified into just one form -pure energy. As the universe spread out and cooled energy began to decrease and mass began to increase toward rest-mass. Matter formed, gravity developed and started clumping matter (mass) together to form structures in the universe as we know it today.

Therefore, you are star dust, a being of light. Every atom and every sub atomic particle is made of light. You are light slowed down. You are part of the electromagnetic system which is a tiny range of all possible frequencies. Science believes that this spectrum is only 0.005% of what actually exists. They call the rest, the known unknowns; these are things they predict exist, like the Higgs Boson or "God particle" that holds all matter together. Then there are the unknown, unknowns that have yet to be predicted or found.
Simply imagine what is just out of your reach, your senses and grasp because at this moment it cannot be detected or perceived.

Light is a vibration and is part of the electromagnetic spectrum. It ranges from the slowest vibrations of radio to the ultra short or fast gamma rays. By changing your thoughts, which are also vibrations, you change not only all aspects of your life, relationships and everything you perceive outside of you, but also you alter every cell and the very DNA structure of the body.

Each cell, too, is made of light and has its own vibration and intelligence which is affected by your moods and how you think and feel. Your heart has a huge magnetic field, even more so than that of the brain.

In fact it is one hundred times electrically stronger and five thousand times magnetically stronger than the brain. This is important as this electromagnetic field makes up your reality wherein you exist. It is your heart that feels your emotions first and not the brain. It can independently process and make its own decisions. These signals are then sent to the brain and affect your emotions and ultimately your health and reality.

Therefore it is vital that you listen to what your heart is telling you and not to the brain. So thinking positively, having kind and loving thoughts towards yourself and others, changes your physiology and affects your well being.

The quickest route to change any aspect of your life is to change the relationship you have with yourself. The more energy you give to a belief system the more you help create that reality.

All journeys start and end within you and are determined by how much you love, respect and care for yourself. The more you value your true worth, the more you can love and see the value of others.

Realise that your judgement of others is only a projection of yourself and your fears. Ask yourself what is it that this judgement, fear or anger is saying about yourself? What are the feelings and emotions you need to look at and deal with?

The more love and understanding that you give to others the more you will receive in return!

The love of the self is an accurate measure of your understanding, your compassion and your humility towards those who demonstrate none.

"For all one's gifts and achievements that transpire over a life time, the greatest gift and achievement of all is the love of the self! When you acquire this you become aware of your own power and immortality and that of everyone and everything else!"

Tuning In

So how do you tune in to your sat nav? Well, the "factory" settings you began your journey with are always up and running.

It is only when you let the street guidance interfere with it does it start leading you down blind alleys. The street guidance, the influence that you pick up on your journey is not always the best directions or co-ordinates to use.

Keep putting in the same co-ordinates and references then you'll keep coming back to the same destination
.

It is when you keep finding yourself in the same set of circumstances, relationships, stuck in the same spot, unable to move on or become ill, that you might then realise it's time to change the frequency you are on and decide on a different route or road to take.

The factory settings or inner voice are always trying to get through all of the other clutter that helps confuse you.

How often do you hear yourself say, "I knew I should have done this instead of that"? "Gone here instead of there" only to realise when it's far too late?

That is your inner guidance (sat nav) trying to get through to you.

Ask yourself when was the last time you sat down in silence? When do you ever give yourself time and space to listen to the silence within you? When was the last time you tuned into your body and listened to what those aches and pains are telling you? When you start to pay attention to all the wonderful insights your mind, body and spirit is trying to communicate to you, then you'll be tuned into your "your higher self!"

So take out the ear phones, switch off the mobile phone and turn off the TV.

It is important to take time out of your day, to let go of the stress and the pressure life puts you under, to listen to these directions.

This can be done by letting go of all the chatter inside your head and to sit quietly without any distraction, meditate or just go for a walk and clear your thoughts!

You will find that when you quieten your mind of the chatter and do this on a regular basis, the doubt and fears you experience will go and the reassurance you need will be there if you just stop and listen to what your heart, your guidance, is actually telling you.

Remember you are not your thoughts but the silence that speaks between them.

Realise this and soon you will be back in harmony and on the right track and your balance restored. It may be hard at first but practice makes perfection!

Also tune into your body, what are those aches and pains really trying to communicate to you? Are they saying, "slow down" "speed up" "more exercise" "stop smoking" "ease up on the alcohol" "cut down on the amount food you eat" "better nutrition"? You know all those things we tend to ignore until the body can no longer cope and decides to make you sit up and take notice with illness, pain, disease and discomfort.
No one else can give you an answer or the peace of mind you are looking for. There is nothing outside of you that can make you happy. The source of happiness and fulfilment lies within. You are the source you are looking for to be happy and to be at peace!

"Wisdom lies in the stillness within"

Changing Position

As you create your journey there will be many other souls or "co creators" with you. Some may agree whole heartedly with what you do or say and other souls may disagree, doubt or totally disregard who they really are.

Don't be fooled by how much passion they put into this belief. It is only their fear of being alone and separate from the divine source that drives them on their way. Also it is because they see the world through the narrow view of the five senses.

As you have seen, you experience such a tiny amount of the universe through the narrow band of the electromagnetic system.

If you think about the diversity of life on this planet and what you experience with such narrow perception, just imagine what else may be just out of the frequency range of these senses.

Some people may play significant parts in your life and stay with you for many of the ups and downs of the trip. Others will stay for part of the journey and some will pass almost unnoticed.

Though don't be mistaken into believing that any are more or less significant than the other. It is not always the quantity of time spent with someone that counts but the quality they may add to your journey and experience.

Sometimes it's the little unexpected things that turn up that will affect and change you the most profoundly.

You are a divine process of light and love and consciousness continually processing, expanding and recreating who you think you are!

So always be prepared to change your position.

Nothing in this world holds fast. Everyone experiences loss and, when it happens, it can seem like there is no way to go forward and nowhere to turn.

Whether it is the loss of a loved one, a relationship, a job, your shares crash, or you become homeless.

Whatever happens, reason not why change occurs but grasp it with both hands. For what may appear as a tragedy can ultimately be the dawn of a golden new age for you.

To undertake each journey you must first change your position, your stance and your way of thinking.

Even the longest of journeys begin with the first step.

Change may come at a price but it also comes as a gift or opportunity to grow and expand your consciousness.

"Just like the waves upon the sea, what is was meant to be. Why try to rearrange? The only constant thing is change!"

Determining Current Position

Scientists believe that the universe works in perfect harmony and balance and if it was out by a tiny fraction it would all collapse.
So you can be sure you are currently in the right time, the right place and correct position at any given moment.
This you have chosen on many levels and through many lives and experiences to be exactly where you are now!
It also stems from the fact that all our actions are determined by two factors -love and fear.

Ask yourself, "Are my choices, decisions, relationships based on love? Giving and receiving in equal measure?"
Are they based knowing that you are infinite love and always connected to source? Or are they based on fears such as lack, self worth, am I good enough? Am I worthy? Can I cope if this happens or that happens?

Never regret where you may have been or come from or why you made the choices you did. That is past.

You will tend to construct and view your present experiences by what has happened to you in the past. Therefore you will react to new experiences the same old way as before. That is until you change the way you view past experiences. By letting go of them and any judgments they can be treated as new experiences, as unique, and you are then free to react differently to similar situations.
It is easier to see these as problems outside of yourself when really they are of your own creation. If you find yourself in a dark place or in fear, then embrace that fear head on.

Only when facing your deepest fears do you find your hidden depths and resources? Your wisdom and strengths are far greater than the limits you put upon yourself.

When you find yourself in darkness it is a chance for your light to shine. Notice! It's only when you stop searching do you find the answer directly in front of you. Only when you stop looking do you cease to be blind and see what you have been looking for and only when you stop your constant chatter do you find the words you need to speak.

We are not the chatter inside our heads nor are we the labels we or other people give ourselves.
We are the silence within. This is our consciousness. This silence does not have to speak as it is all knowing.

When we listen to this silence within it is then we get the answers we are longing for.

If the Universe really is perfectly constructed, mathematically sound right down to the tiniest particle as scientists say, then no matter how insignificant you may think you are or you may feel your life to be at times, just remember that without you in the complexity of the whole equation then the universe would become unstable and the whole sum of the universe would not add up or be complete!

"Only when you stop searching will you find your way
Only when you stop talking will you know what to say
Only when you stop looking will you cease to be blind
Only when you start listening will the answers you find"

The Imaginary Journey

Where you are today is a direct result of your past thoughts and past actions. The person you are going to be is created out of the thoughts you now have and actions you now do. Most people sow their thoughts like a gardener, randomly sowing seed using the open cast method. The thoughts, like the seed, are scattered and left by chance to be buffeted by the breeze and fall aimlessly to the ground before they can take root and grow. By thinking this way you are left open to have your life fashioned by other people and circumstances. Instead it really is important to focus and be aware of each and every thought.

Everything that man has created was once just a thought or idea in the mind of its creator. The chair you sit on, the TV you watch, the music you listen to, the car you drive, the house you live in, everything! If man is capable of creating these things out of thoughts, then what else can you do to help create your experience? Instead of thinking randomly, or wishing for a certain outcome, what if you direct your thoughts intentionally? Remember nothing is real or stays the same; only your perception of what you think is real.

Take away emotion from a thought and it has no power! Give only your attention to the thoughts and things which you wish to allow into your experience.
What you believe to be real and what you give your attention and focus to becomes your reality!
Every time you use statements such as "I am" you are making a statement about your belief of who you are to your subconscious mind and to the universe. You are telling them how you perceive yourself and how much value you place upon yourself. If you continually repeat sentences such as "I can't" then sure enough you won't, say "I am this or I am that" and sure enough you are! Say "I always end up with the same kind of partner who treats me badly" and guess what - you do. Keep saying "I could never ever be …" and you never will or ever shall be. The list goes on and on. If you say "I am" make sure it is a positive statement about who you are. Start to say "I can" then you will. Start to believe that you can and then anything becomes possible! This is because every time you make a statement over and over again it gets ingrained into the subconscious mind, and the subconscious will do everything it can in connection with the universe to make it become your reality and attract those things to you, even though you may not desire them. This is how the Law of Attraction works.

What you think you create!

"If you are without then change what lies within!"

Laws of the journey

Governing Law

The reality of who you truly are is a soul, a being of infinite possibilities, part of a universal consciousness having an experience being human. This may take place over many life times until you decide that there is nothing left for you to experience. There are no limitations placed upon you, only the ones you place upon yourself. As being a human is for such a relatively short period, and you being part of the greater eternal consciousness, it is safe to assume that being in the human condition is just like having a dream. That dream seems real while you're in it but when you awaken it quickly fades. You realise it was just an illusion that you experience from time to time in different bodies playing out many roles and is just part of an ongoing universal process.

Soul Contracts

It is not unusual for souls to make contracts to meet again in other life times. These can be individual souls who plan to come together again to perhaps fulfil tasks together. Lovers can be re united to fulfil their dreams. Families can return to take on different roles whereby they choose to be a different gender, sibling or parent. Often people speak of having a soul partner. This is usually another person we feel a great bond or resonance with. In truth, of course, we are all soul partners as we are all part of the one source.

Law of Attraction

It is only by being aware of what you are thinking and the words you are using that you can begin to make significant alterations to your journey.
The outer reality is based upon your inner belief systems of who you think you are. Change your thoughts and you change your outer reality.
There are many physical laws that we take for granted such as the law of gravity but until Isaac Newton recognised it and explained its properties no one understood it. So too, it is the same with recognising the law of attraction and how it creates and manifests conditions and situations in your life.
This law creates your experiences through the vibration of thought and attracts to what you give your intention to and the equal amount of emotion you put behind your thoughts.

Always be conscious of the thoughts you are putting "out there". Remember the old saying, "be careful what you wish for."

Your thoughts are vibrations. All matter is vibration and your thoughts are continually creating, manifesting and attracting experiences into your journey via the divine Matrix.

Imagination is the motion of mind and should not to be confused with daydreaming which is just random thoughts.

When you use your imagination and place your attention, intention and emotion upon it, you start creating who you want to be, where you want to go, what you want to do and what you want to achieve.

You can then focus and use your imagination to bring about the desired result.

Picture how you will go about it, the tools you need to fashion it, how it will look and feel when you have it.

Above all believe and be congruent with the outcome you desire. All conscious actions are preceded by a thought.

Ask yourself; are your thoughts constructive or obstructive? Negative or are they positive? Do they continually put you down? Raise or lower your expectations?

There is only one way to change the experiences you are having in your life and that is by changing your thoughts and the way you think about them. Change the way you think and you will change the way you act. Change the way you act and you will experience different results.

You have free will to choose, at any given moment, to change who you are, where you want to be.

The Law of Karma

This is the universal law of action and reaction.

It is not a punishment. It is just a reflection of not only all your thoughts, deeds and actions but, through our genes and DNA, the thoughts fears and actions of our ancestors. "As you sow, so you shall reap." "What goes round comes round" are two common expressions of this law in motion.

By forgiving ourselves and the actions of others and of our ancestors we can break the cycle of karma.

Whatever you do, say, or think has a resonance, a vibration and power and ultimately has an effect on you and your outer reality.

These vibrations will at some time reflect back upon you and you'll have to face the consequences of those thoughts and actions.

Sometimes the karma or consequence of your actions is instant and at other times it may take place over many life times.

Karma is just another tool through which you can experience, during each of your life times, the full circle of all possibilities. By being rich, poor, saint, sinner, victor, loser, deaf, dumb, blind, lame, male and female, plus all colours, hues and creeds.

Think of it as more of an educational experience rather than any sort of punishment.
After all, you are choosing your different lifetimes so that you cover every aspect and condition of the human experience and once you are outside the cycle of life experiences karma doesn't exist. In "reality" you are an eternal entity and being human is only a very temporary condition.

By forgiving yourself and the actions of others and of our ancestors you can break and let go of the cycle of karma you are in.

"Beyond each journey awaits yet another, even greater one which you all must take. To become part of the vast ocean of what you all are, pure love, consciousness and all that is, ever was and always shall be."

Limiting Your Options

For centuries man's options were limited by the information he received. Unlike today, where communication is instant and we know what is taking place on the other side of the planet without even going outside our front door.

By comparison our ancestors had to wait weeks or months to hear what was happening in the world. Most people would never even travel outside of their towns or villages. Very little would change in their world throughout their lives. So their choices, options and experiences were much more limited.

Over the last two hundred years change has become the norm for us. Since the industrial revolution our journey has been accelerating. Major changes in technology that would have taken decades in the past now seem to be happening every day. Information is all around us and access to it has never been easier or faster.

This ultimately gives us greater choice and freedom. So there is never a need to limit yourself or your options as change is always taking place and you are part of that constant change. Indeed perhaps it is not change we fear the most but staying the same or continually being in the same situation.

There is always more than one road to take to achieve the goals and outcomes you desire and to overcome any difficulties you may face on your journey. It is said that there are no problems only solutions, though sometimes the problem may seem to be finding a solution.
.
Your reality or how you perceive it can be changed by a thought in an instant. A person may stand beside you facing the same set of circumstances but will ultimately be seeing a different view and perspective than you and will experience totally different thoughts and emotions. Remember most of your limitations and responses are pre-programmed into your subconscious mind from an early age. So you may conveniently limit yourself from creating the change you desire by using your relationships, financial position, religion, insecurity, prescription drugs or fears for the future.

Whatever it is you may feel that keeps you from reaching your true magnificent creative self, there are always options and choices you can make to change any circumstance and situation.

Sometimes people will even try to limit each other's experiences because they fear that if someone close to them changes it will mean they have to change too and this will bring them out of their comfort zone.

This is because although they may be unhappy where they are and they feel stuck, or perhaps know it is an unhealthy place to be, some people resist change because they are afraid of what the unknown may bring. You can blame everyone else for the exact position you find yourself in but the fact is, you are where you are right now because of the choices and actions that you made in the past.

It is easier to blame others than to try to understand them. It is easier to criticise somebody else than it is to look at yourself and your own actions and the consequences.

By showing yourself more love and understanding you can create and transform your life and the road you take.

"Whoever you may think you are or believe yourself to be, you are always far greater, more powerful and more magnificent than you can ever imagine!"

Intended Destination

Some people know from an early age what they want to be or the direction they want to go in. Others find themselves being blown and buffeted by whatever life may throw at them.

To find your intended destination, let go of luck and chance and circumstance. Be still and listen to your inner guidance. It is always there to guide you.

Remember the subconscious mind drives you forward, the conscious mind makes the decisions and the higher consciousness guides you if you allow yourself to listen to it.

This higher consciousness has all the known resources of the universe to guide and help you achieve your goals. You can use these resources at any given time to let go of any limiting patterns, beliefs or behaviours that may be holding you back.

The "secret" most people keep from themselves is that they are far greater and more powerful than they can ever imagine or think possible.

As you now know thought creates. You can always change and create the person you want to be or believe yourself to be at any given moment.

To get to where you want to go you have to be congruent with what you desire and want to create. That means not only thinking and speaking of where you want to be, and where you want get to, but also thinking, being, doing and acting upon the thoughts and words.

All thoughts and actions should be in the present tense, as don't forget, if you keep saying "I want" then you will always be wanting. Instead, thank the universe for giving you what it is your heart desires as if you have already received it!

Your entire focus should be on the things that inspire you to this aim. If you make a plan or write a list of what is needed and you find yourself not acting upon something, ask yourself what it is about you that is holding you back. Is it the fear of change, fear of failure or even the fear of being successful? There is no point putting in little effort and expecting great results.

Take a world class athlete who dedicates themselves to train year in year out just to run, swim or jump in one Olympic final that may take only seconds to complete.

Their whole focus, being and energy is on that one goal. So be aware that you are limitless, undying consciousness capable of achieving anything that you wish to focus your attention upon.

"To look for the divine in another is the surest way not to see it.

To recognise it is within your self is the only way to experience it"

Making Changes

The only constant in the universe, of course, is change. Yet people all the time try to hold onto things when they no longer serve them. It is their attachment to these things that gives them value. Whether it is material objects, money, relationships, places or emotions, by not letting go they ultimately cause them pain.

It is only your will or ego that stubbornly holds onto the belief that when change occurs in your life without your consent it is bad for you because you feel out of control and therefore it leaves you in fear.

By accepting everything must ultimately change then you can allow it to pass quickly. The speed at which it occurs is ultimately up to you. Change is always just a thought away.

Thoughts on their own have no power, of course, unless you place emotion behind them. Then they can be turned into action. This process can change you and all around you in an instant. Constantly you are being bombarded with negative thoughts and images. When you watch the TV news, listen to the radio, read a newspaper or pick up a magazine, you are told what to think and how to act and react even though you are told these are just news STORIES we forget that's just what they are, STORIES.

Even the drugs we take and the additives and chemicals in the processed foods and the fluoride in the water we drink, change the way we behave and think, cloud our judgment as well as affect our well being!

Governments are happy while the majority of the people are following their consensus and agenda, even encouraging other nationalities to demand more freedom and more rights. When suddenly confronted by the majority of its own people becoming disenchanted and starting to demand change a government will panic and try to suppress the will of its people, even more than usual, by calling them unpatriotic or anarchic minority, and bring in draconian laws or even resort to violence.

Fortunately, history has shown us as with Ghandi in India, the communist block after the Second World War and now in Egypt, Syria, Libya and many other African states, that once thought and action become as one nothing can hold back the seeds of change. All change begins with us, not with a revolution.

Even as I write, there are protests on Wall Street New York, London, Madrid, Athens and other major cities around the western world as people tire of an old outdated system which keeps millions in poverty while the few prosper.

When people realise their own power and the consciousness of the people changes then there is very little a government can do to prevent change.

So it is with personal growth. Once you realise that you are the creator of your universe, and consciousness creates through you, then you can make decisions to change and focus upon what it is you really desire.

Take action and the whole universe will move in your favour, opening doors, setting up meetings, events, people and what appears to be coincidences.

Taking action creates the momentum for all manner of things to happen.

*"Sometimes you can be further from your destination
In your final step than you were in your first"*

New co-ordinates

So how do you change direction? You are being given guidance continually on your journey as to where you should go or what decisions to take. Sometimes that guidance will be very subtle, like a feeling, a longing, or a knowing. Other times it will hit you smack in the face like a sledge hammer, changing your life dramatically, through death, divorce or an accident. Other times it can be a chance meeting, a book you read or something small that turns up out of the blue that makes you think differently and changes your life path forever.

When reading a book, are you really reading what the author is trying to convey to you or is it just your interpretation of what the author wanted to get across?
When standing in an art gallery is it the painting or the artist that really speaks to you or again, how you interpret what you are seeing?
As you have seen you are the co-creator of all that is in your reality and along with all the other people whom you meet on the journey, everything has an influence no matter how great or small.

Once you are given a different view of how to read, view, value or interpret something in a new way then your opinion, your mind and your reality are changed forever. Likewise your co-ordinates are being finely tuned all the time, to see things differently and to make the subtle changes you need to.

You are always being made aware of what you need to know. Although quite often, if you're not finely tuned into your Sat Nav, when these things are presented to you you'll ignore them until at a later date you realise you should have listened or taken note of those feelings you were getting.

Nothing that appears in your life is by chance or coincidence. Everything is as it should be. You are never given a challenge that you are not ready for, or able to cope or deal with, without being given an opportunity to solve it or grow through it.

No matter how great something may appear, or how distant and out of reach the stars may seem to be, or how deep the oceans may lie, within you is the key to unlock any mystery no matter how great it may appear to be.

Speed Zones

While on your journey you may feel that time is speeding up, everything seems to be happening much quicker than before. This is partly due to the fact that for centuries relatively small amounts of information and facts were collected. Those facts and information were limited to a few people in power and kept from away the masses.

Now every day we are being opened up to and bombarded with new knowledge and facts from many different sources. According to the Encyclopaedia Britannica, since the ancient Sumerians' time zone around 3,800 BC to 1900 AD, only a relatively small amount of knowledge was collected. From 1900 to 1950 our knowledge then doubled. In the following 20 years our knowledge doubled again and in the next 10 years it doubled again.

Another reason that time seems to be quickening is because of a wobble in the earth's rotation called the procession of the Equinox. This happens once every 26,920 years. It means that the Earth is pointing into the centre of the galaxy where there is amassed the greatest amount consciousness and we are picking up on this. The exact time for the alignment with the universe is of the 21st December 2012 .This is the date of the end of the Mayan calendar! It does not predict the end of the world, as many people believe, but the end of a cycle or era. We are entering the Age of Aquarius where instead of being governed by the male left brain we will instead be governed more by the female right brain. This in turn will give us more compassion, understanding and willingness to express ourselves through arts and literature and less inclined to want to solve difficulties with anger, discord and violence.

*"If the caterpillar feared the future,
It may never know the beauty of the
Butterfly!"*

Advanced settings

Besides the basic settings of tuning in to find guidance there are more advanced ones you can use which shamans and healers have used for thousands of years to help heal the body.

As you have learned, you are part of a collective consciousness. Nothing is separate. To manifest anything into your reality first you must give it thought, emotion, then intent and then action.

When a healing occurs which is outside the conventional medical paradigm and doctors have no explanation for what has happened, they say that, spontaneous healings happen! Or it must be the placebo effect! That's fine, but it never explains or tries to explain how it happens.

It is the same when one travels to ancient sites around the world and see buildings constructed with huge stones weighing many hundreds of tons and statues so symmetrically carved that even modern day techniques, tools and machinery would be hard to move or fashion them.

Yet scholars still insist that they were moved and created with rudimentary stone tools by hand.

Very rarely do they try to demonstrate how their theory could possibly work on a practical basis.

So too doctors tend to dismiss anything that is outside their understanding. We know that the body is fantastic at healing itself and we are aware sometimes it is helped greatly by surgery or drugs.

At other times though alternative methods can be used with greater effect to fine tune the mind body and spirit with the use of such methods as hypnosis, EFT, Reiki, spiritual healing, distant healing, acupuncture, past life regression and so on. The list is endless.

Remember you are a being of light vibrating at a cellular level. When you experience trauma, sadness, anger and many of the other ups and downs and emotions that life brings you literally hold onto those emotions and they resonate within the body on some level. If they are not released or dealt with they create illness.

By changing your frequency through healing or changing your thoughts you begin to free the energy blocks from the physical, mental, spiritual and emotional levels and the body can then get on with the job of healing itself. So how do you access these settings? Like a lot of other things it has been suggested that only if you are someone special, or have trained for years in a discipline, or are with a certain organisation or hold a certification can you be a healer. That may be so with some of the techniques and disciplines but really everyone is a natural healer if they allow themselves to be.

On a simple level most parents experience this when their child falls or hurts themselves, they will kiss or rub the injured area "to make it better". At other times it can just be a comforting arm around a friend or a sympathetic ear for a loved one.

The so called more advanced levels can be accessed, for example, by a simple prayer asking the higher consciousness for healing.
Distant healing can be used when a person is not in your presence. This is done by asking the divine consciousness for healing and picturing the person who needs it being recovered, looking fit and well.

Hands on healing (such as spiritual healing and Reiki) is done by placing ones hands on or over the person who requires it and again asking for healing energy to pass through you to the person.

What they, and all methods of healing, have in common is the thought, love and intent by which it is given. As we are all connected on this level of vibration we really can affect each other's energy this way and help people recover from illness by "tuning in" and asking for it to be so.

"Each step you take on your journey is another step closer to the divine within you! All!"

Gratitude

It is by giving our gratitude and our thanks to all we have met and all we have experienced on this journey that truly sets us free.

Once we feel gratitude we are no longer in fear, guilt, doubt or lack anything. Remember, without those other souls who have impacted on our lives, no matter how great or small, there would have been no journey and no experience to help us grow and expand our consciousness.

It helps not to hold onto anger, jealousy, hatred or the fear that you may have endured.

If someone is critical of you it is only a reflection of them, their fears and their perception of you.

Whilst it is common to experience many different emotions, they only weigh us down. The quicker you release them the quicker and easier you will proceed on the journey. Gratitude, after all, raises our vibration.

It connects us with our higher self and helps change our outer world and so should be a daily routine not just for the receiving of a tangible gift or a small act of kindness.

You should be grateful for the many different blessings you receive, rather than focusing on the negative.

It releases you from being a victim and living your future from past hurt and discomfort, and allows you to define yourself by how much you have grown.

After all, there is no future in the past. It is with forgiveness and gratitude that you allow peace and harmony into your life.

By giving thanks to past experiences and people you are opening yourself up to abundance and the depth and beauty the universe gives to us each and every day.

Forgiveness

Forgiveness heals the spiritual, mental, physical and emotional levels of being. It frees you from being bound by past actions and liberates you to move forward on your journey in peace and in harmony.

You can then create your journey from the present, instead of from the past!

Forgiveness means letting go all feelings of injustice, sorrow, pain, resentment and revenge. Thus you are able to move forward with love and a lightness of heart.

There is no dishonour in letting go, only courage and the belief that you are worthy of so much more!

To forgive is the key to open the door to your own happiness. It leaves room for something new and wonderful to fill the void you have created by letting go!

This is the time of your life; do not be held back by any thoughts of resentment, nor anyone nor anything.

The gift of forgiveness is in your hands - give it with love and you will set yourself free to face new experiences without judgement of yourself or others!

"Never underestimate the gift of love
It has no demands!"

Which journey to take?

Which journey or what road should you choose to take? Well, of course, that's just it; there is no journey to take, no distance to travel and nowhere you need to go.

There is nothing to search for. There is no one for you to seek out to give you an answer. Everything, all knowledge lies within you. Though you may feel you are on a journey you are always exactly where you are meant, and choose, to be. You are neither here nor there but everywhere! Yet still some people believe that leaving no stone unturned, reading yet another book, seeing the next film, travelling the world, visiting the right Guru, attending the next workshop, will allow them to tune into the secret or get the answer they are searching for.

When actually the truth is, there is no place you have to be. Put the emphasis on life's experiences rather than life's purpose.

The answer and truth you seek is right here, within you. This is where you need to look. It is not outside of you. No one else can give it to you. The magic formula, the answer for the love, peace of mind and wisdom you are craving, you already have. You are the magician.

There is nothing that is outside of you that can make you happy! The source of all happiness, wisdom and fulfilment lies within you.

You are the source of everything you are looking and searching for, and when you realise there is no journey that awaits you, nowhere to go, no answer to find, it is then you will know that in fact,

YOU ARE THE JOURNEY ITSELF!

Yes, that's right. Sorry if you didn't get it, but it's all an illusion. You may question who am I? Or state, I am this or that. I am male or I am female! I am young or old! I am my emotions or my feelings! Whatever you may think, you are not these thoughts.

You are the source, the thinker behind the thought. The idea of who you are is just your attachment to those thoughts and throughout your life time your thoughts and the idea of who you believe yourself to be will continually change too.

Just as your body changes, your attachments to people, places and the idea of that which you think you are will change too, as you experience new things and meet different people.

You are a culmination of all experiences that have ever existed and that will continue to exist.

You are all the words you have ever heard and spoken, the emotions you have felt, the tears of joy and sadness, the love you have touched and lost! Yet you are beyond all these things and more.

Not only are you the one within the One; the one who observes the thoughts and experiences. The truth of who you are is beyond all these things, you are beyond belief, beyond definition and trying to define who you are only diminishes your being.

You are no less than existence and awareness itself! When one attains this understanding you realise there are no you, I or self. You are consciousness itself!

As you prepare to move into and create your future out of the now, this present moment, it is only if you can recognise your infinite wisdom that you can reach your palace of possibilities, your potential to create the things you desire in life, which are always just a thought away. You are the true creator and master of this small space that you inhabit, in what is the vastness of a conscious universe.

"I think, therefore I am and whatever has entered my mind is in truth the illusion of my dreams" said the Greek philosopher Descartes.

"I am that I am" spoke God to Moses in the Old Testament.

Was this in truth not telling you that whatever you think you are, or when you state "I am", then so surely you become?

Restrictions of use

You are born into this illusion of reality with your own ideas and paradigms.

From an early age you are taught to think in a predetermined way as to what is and what can be.

Education and society teaches you to think like everyone else, to conform to that which is accepted by the majority and not to question what you are being told.

This system that not only constricts you by the laws and information it gives you, but is policed by everyone else in the system, by their condemnation of anyone who thinks or acts differently from the rest of that society.

This is a system where half the population die of hunger and most of the rest die or suffer disease from over eating.

In this system our wealth is judged not by the depth of our love and compassion but by our monetary wealth, status and education.

Terms and conditions

So what are the terms and conditions for being on this journey? I don't believe that there are any. I feel we are well prepared before we get here. Just as we may pass our driving test, that is only the beginning of the process. It is only by being on the road and experiencing different situations and conditions that we become more experienced, competent and accomplished as drivers.

There is no judgment other than that which is given by other people and that which we place upon ourselves! There is no heaven or hell, no angry God or deity that awaits us. How could there be if God is love? Perhaps if there is any judgement it's just our own interpretation of what we have experienced; though I'm sure that after leaving this earth plane, being shown the bigger picture and given hind sight, I don't really think there would be any need of guilt at all.

Our thoughts are living things that create our experiences. The more energy and intent we give to them then the more they construct and weave the tapestry of our lives. Therefore the reality around us consistently conforms to our beliefs and the expectations we have! If someone says, when talking of relationships, "I always seem to meet the wrong person for me" or "nothing I ever do goes right", then that is what they experience. People who are successful have a different paradigm on the way they see things. They expect to be successful. If something doesn't work the first time they don't see it as failure but they will try some different way until it does eventually work out.

The people and situations we draw into our lives are there because we have attracted them to us on some level for experience.

When people meet they interact not just on a physical level but on a conscious, subconscious vibration and energetic level. Their auras meet and interact, exchanging information that conforms to and reinforces the other person's view of their reality.

We all get that feeling sometimes when we walk into a room and it feels uncomfortable; or it feels really good. This is because we are picking up on other people's vibrations.

We can even feel this in an empty room because of the vibrations that are left there. This is because we are not confined to this physical body. There is no one in here, as such. We are everywhere at once. The only limitations are the ones we place upon ourselves.

Ownership and Responsibility

By owning and taking responsibility and giving gratitude for everything in your life - your body, emotions, feelings, fears, fantasies, dreams, aspirations, insights, successes, failures, hopes, words, thoughts, highs, lows, gains, losses and all your actions, you are opening up to fully understanding who you really are. As this realisation grows it allows you to transform and to be more loving and kind to yourself for all that which has gone before and all that you have yet to experience.

Owning, taking responsibility and giving gratitude for all aspects of yourself allows you to be free to forgive all that has been experienced by you and then discard, without judgment or prejudice any aspects which you dislike or now find inappropriate and no longer serve you. This leaves you able to replace it with something new and truly magnificent.

By doing this you open yourself and your senses up to the world that is inside of you and that which you perceive to be outside of you. It allows you not only to be more loving, tolerant and understanding towards others as they express themselves, but, above all it allows you to expand and fully express who you really are!

You are, after all, who you have chosen to be. All past decisions you made have brought you into the present space that you now occupy. In this world there is no one else like you.

You are unique and all that stems from you is of your design and making and contains this uniqueness.

Miscellaneous

So the Satellite Navigational System to your Soul has reminded you that there is no journey.

You are always where you are meant to be by the decisions and choices you have made.

You are part of the ultimate consciousness occupying a human body, experiencing what you perceive as a journey.

Yet you continually put yourself down by giving labels to your experiences and judging them and yourself as being good or bad instead of accepting that, whatever happened it just is or was, without adding the labels.

As you go through your experiences and they bring out the different emotions within you, instead of giving labels to them you should ask, "What is it in me that makes me feel like this or makes me react in a particular way?" It is only when you don't face up to, or hold onto, these emotions that they then can create imbalances within your body and your mind, which ultimately lead you and your body out of sync. It is when the body is out of balance that you become more prone to illness and disease.

What you attract into your life is controlled by the vibrations you give off. These vibrations are controlled by your emotions and intentions, both by the thoughts you are aware of in your conscious mind and those you are unaware of in your subconscious mind.

What you call "your reality" is, in fact, just energy. It is a collection of atoms and cells that oscillate at a particular frequency and then act and interact with the world outside of us.

Your brain interprets the world as being real when in fact what you see and experience are just electrical signals or vibrations that your brain decodes and we construe as being real.

As you are energy and vibration this connects us to everything. Ultimately what you do affects everything and everyone around us.

The oldest religions and philosophies have always proclaimed this oneness!

It is only now through quantum physics that science is catching up with the notion that everything is connected.

Charles Darwin, who outlined his Theory of Evolution in his book (and remember it's still only a theory) "On the Origin of Species" in 1859, stated that in nature there was a natural selection process, the Survival of the Fittest. Yet countless studies have shown that nature works best when it is in harmony with everything else and not in competition.

After all, considering that there are over seven billion people on earth it's amazing that the majority do live in peace, harmony and co-operation.

Scientists, because of this theory have been looking for what they call the missing link between us Homo sapiens and our so called immediate ancestors Homo erectus and Homo heidelbergenis. They over look the fact that we suddenly appeared on Earth about 200,000 years ago and have never found a shred of evidence or DNA connecting us with them at all.

This is just another example of main stream science trying to put together the pieces of a puzzle that will never fit because they stubbornly refuse to accept any other possibilities.

Disclaimer

So here is your Satellite Navigation Guide to Your Soul to help you remember who you are and why you are here on this so called journey.
.

By thinking "outside the box" and not accepting everything we are told in text books and the media we can tune into our higher selves and remain open to all life's possibilities.
If we remain open, then, what once seemed impossible just might become an everyday occurrence.

Of course none of what is written in this book may be true or real. Perhaps it is just an illusion, a figment of my imagination!
It's for you to know and create what is, after all, your reality and how ultimately, you perceive it!

"You will find the deeper you delve the more mysteries you will uncover. Create only that which you need and not that which you want. Remember you may amass great wealth but you will never own it. For material objects are only in your possession for a short time before they pass unto someone else.

The most valuable commodity you will ever have is the love of the self and for others. Do not be drawn into other people's plans, or dramas. Always choose your own way. The more you learn and the more you understand, the more you can let go of. The more you let go of the more that will open up to you. It is our attachment to people places and material objects that cause us pain! Take life in your stride for each step will bring you closer to your destination. Illusion is a distraction to those who will sleep walk through their lives. Deception is the art with which fools delude themselves and get others to believe.

There is only one truth. That which transcends all things and all worlds, love. It guides you home to where all souls rest and all are nourished in its pool of infinite light and wisdom. Be the light you are seeking and you will shine upon this earth as a beacon of love and hope for everyone else to behold."

Lament for those who have left this vibration

Grieve not at my passing for I am at peace and as one
Mourn only the things that remain undone

The seed of love that has yet to be sown
The hand of friendship to he who casts a stone

Reveal the light inside which is so hard to shine
To those left in the darkness without a sign

Emit the love you find hard to reveal
Feed the child who's in need of a meal

Heal the hearts in need of repair
Be the ray of hope for those in despair

Give an arm of comfort to those in need
And a word of encouragement to help them succeed

Yes grieve not my passing without a tear or a sigh
Eternity views our time here but in the blink of an eye

So don't be sad these days we're apart
Give me just a thought and I'm there in your heart

Pure Love is forever and will never be undone
Yes grieve you not for I am at peace and at one

Colour of Life (Denny Lloyd)

Well I don't know which way to turn because I'm not sure which way I am facing.
Feelings contradict my thoughts, I can't tell what is real or just imagination.
Well don't let me drown? In this world of illusion.
I saw a film it was my life, it was my life and I played the starring role.
Of a man in search of meaning and feeling and the hero inside his soul

What's sleeping inside my soul?

Each day my story it unfolds. Page by page you are turning
And though my story lacks a plot, between the lines is where you will find me.
Time after time, Feel like I'm going in circles.

I saw a film it was my life, it was my life and I played the starring role,
Of a man in search of meaning and feeling and the hero inside his soul
What's sleeping inside my soul?
Because I am searching for something and I been searching for someone and I am searching for somewhere I belong.

And in the film and you see your life, this is your life and you're trying to play a hero.
Our lives move fast in slow motion, slow motion and we're watching it fade away
And in the film that is my life, this is my life and I play the starring role
Of a man who is lucky, he is lucky, though he doesn't realise.
Yeah when will we realise, that we're the heroes of our own lives!

Colour of Life: Lyrics and music by Denny Lloyd ©
From the album "If symptoms persist" visit denny Lloyd on you tube

Available on iTunes visit www.dennylloyd.com

*"The rest of your journey is about to begin.
Each step is an opportunity for you to enhance
and enlighten the life of everyone you meet!"*

Printed in Germany
by Amazon Distribution
GmbH, Leipzig